Over on the Farm

A barnyard baby animal counting book

BY MARIANNE BERKES ILLUSTRATED BY CATHY MORRISON

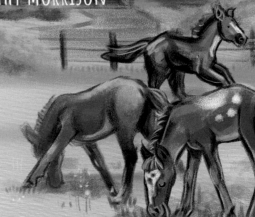

Over on the farm,
in the early morning sun,
lived a busy mother hen
and her little chick **one**.

"Peck," said the mother.
"I peck," said the **one**.
So they pecked on the ground
in the early morning sun.

1

Over on the farm,
where they always have to chew,
lived a mother nanny goat
and her little kids **two**.

"Nibble," said the mother.
"We nibble," said the **two**.
So they nibbled on the grass
that they always have to chew.

Over on the farm,
near a buzzing bumblebee,
lived a spotted mother cow
and her little calves **three**.

"Swish," said the mother.
"We swish," said the **three**.
So they swished with their tails
at the buzzing bumblebee.

3

Over on the farm,
waiting on the barn floor,
lived a clever mother cat
and her little kittens **four**.

"Wash," said the mother.
"We wash," said the **four**.
So they licked themselves clean
waiting on the barn floor.

Over on the farm,
where the corn plants thrive,
lived a graceful mother horse
and her little foals **five**.

"Gallop," said the mother.
"We gallop," said the **five**.
So they galloped by a field
where the corn plants thrive.

Over on the farm,
near a brood of little chicks,
lived a hungry mother mouse
and her little pups **six.**

"Hide," said the mother.
"We hide," said the **six.**
So they hid in the hay
near a brood of little chicks.

6

Over on the farm,
in a tree-hollow heaven,
lived a mother barn owl
and her little owlets **seven**.

"Fly," said the mother.
"We fly," said the **seven**.
So they flew silently
from their tree-hollow heaven.

7

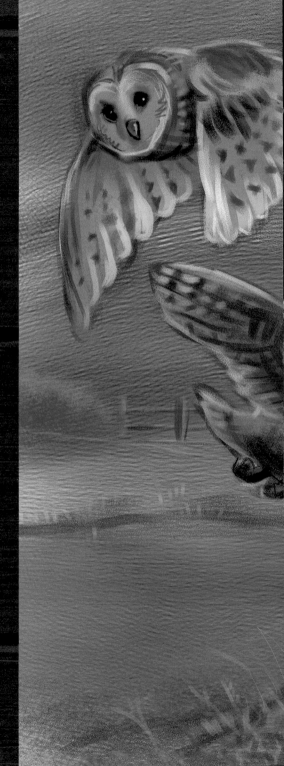

Over on the farm,
near an old barn gate,
lived a noisy mother turkey
and her little poults **eight**.

"Strut," said the mother.
"We strut," said the **eight**.
So they strutted in the straw
near an old barn gate.

Over on the farm,
where they followed in a line,
lived a white mother duck
and her yellow ducklings **nine**.

"Waddle," said the mother.
"We waddle," said the **nine**.
So they waddled to the water
where they followed in a line.

9

Over on the farm,
in a muddy pig pen,
lived a huge mother pig
and her little piglets **ten**.

"Roll," said the mother.
"We roll," said the **ten**.
So they rolled all around
in a muddy pig pen.

10

Over on the farm,
where the baby animals play,
while their mothers all were resting
they up and got away!

"Find us," say the babies,
"from ten to one."
When you count them on this page,
the story isn't done.

Go back to every page
and spy with your eyes.
Do you see the father rooster?
Isn't he a surprise!

10 pigs	5 horses
9 ducks	4 cats
8 turkeys	3 cows
7 owls	2 goats
6 mice	1 chicken

Over on the Farm

Sung to the tune
"Over in the Meadow"

Traditional tune
Words by Marianne Berkes

Soprano

O - ver on the farm, in the ea - rly morn-ing sun, lived a bu - sy mo - ther

S

hen and her lit - tle chick one. "Peck," said the mo-ther. "I peck," said the

S

one. So they pecked on the ground in the ear - ly mor - ning sun.

2. Over on the farm, where they always have to chew,
lived a mother nanny goat and her little kids two.
"Nibble," said the mother. "We nibble," said the two.
So they nibbled on the grass that they always have
to chew.

3. Over on the farm, near a buzzing bumblebee,
lived a spotted mother cow and her little calves three.
"Swish," said the mother. "We swish," said the three.
So they swished with their tails at the buzzing bumblebee.

4. Over on the farm, waiting on the barn floor,
lived a clever mother cat and her little kittens four.
"Wash," said the mother. "We wash," said the four.
So they licked themselves clean waiting on the barn floor.

5. Over on the farm, where the corn plants thrive,
lived a graceful mother horse and her little foals five.
"Gallop," said the mother. "We gallop," said the five.
So they galloped by a field where the corn plants thrive.

6. Over on the farm, near a brood of little chicks,
lived a hungry mother mouse and her little pups six.
"Hide," said the mother. "We hide," said the six.
So they hid in the hay near a brood of little chicks.

7. Over on the farm, in a tree-hollow heaven,
lived a mother barn owl and her little owlets seven.
"Fly," said the mother. "We fly," said the seven.
So they flew silently from their tree-hollow heaven.

8. Over on the farm, near an old barn gate,
lived a noisy mother turkey and her little poults eight.
"Strut," said the mother. "We strut," said the eight.
So they strutted in the straw near an old barn gate.

9. Over on the farm, where they followed in a line,
lived a white mother duck and her little ducklings nine.
"Waddle," said the mother. "We waddle," said the nine.
So they waddled to the water where they followed in
a line.

10. Over on the farm, in a muddy pig pen,
lived a huge mother pig and her little piglets ten.
"Roll," said the mother. "We roll," said the ten.
So they rolled all around in a muddy pig pen.

Fact or Fiction?

In this farm adaptation of "Over in the Meadow" by Olive A. Wadsworth, the animals really do peck, gallop, and waddle as they have been portrayed, but the number of babies they have is very different. That is fiction!

Here are the facts: Cows and horses usually have one baby and goats have two. Cats have litters of four to six kittens, while pigs often have ten piglets in a litter, and mice have even more. Hens raise as many as twelve chicks at a time. Barn owls usually have five to seven owlets in a clutch, and turkeys and ducks lay as many as eight to ten eggs.

Nature has very different ways of ensuring the survival of different species. Cows, goats, horses, cats, pigs and mice all nurse their babies after they are born, some for as long as two years. Ducklings and chicks bond with their mothers as soon as they hatch. In the case of the barn owl, both parents are fully involved in rearing their young.

Seasons on the Farm

A farm is a place where fruits, vegetables, and grains are grown. Some animals are raised for milk, eggs, or meat. Activities on the farm change throughout the seasons.

SPRING - This is the time when most baby animals are born. As the sun warms the Earth, new grass appears, and horses and cows are put out to pasture. Fields are fertilized and plowed. Seeds are spread and planted. Cows with babies produce milk, which is sold all throughout the year.

SUMMER - Vegetables and fruits grow and so do baby animals. Corn and hay grow tall, and the hay is raked and baled. Eggs are collected every day. As vegetables ripen, they're sold to be enjoyed by families like yours.

FALL - It's harvest time! The growing season has come to an end, and the last fruits and vegetables are gathered and sold. The silo is filled with corn or other grains that will feed the animals in the winter.

WINTER - The barn is made ready for animals to come inside where it is warmer. Inside, they are given hay and grain to eat. Chickens keep laying eggs and cows are still milked.

About the Animals

Baby **chickens** are called chicks. Hens are female chickens. A mother hen lays her eggs and sits on them for about three weeks to keep them warm until they hatch. She shows her chicks how to use their beaks to peck the ground to look for food in the barnyard.

Baby **goats** are called kids. Goats are almost always chewing. They like to nibble on grass. Their saliva makes food wet enough to swallow, and it goes into one part of the goat's stomach. When that part of the stomach is full, the goat brings up a wad of food and chews it again before it goes into another part of its stomach to be digested.

Baby **cows** are called calves. Cows spend a lot of time in fields where they eat grass. They often swish their tails when insects bother them. Like goats, cows have a special stomach that allows them to cough up a wad of grass or hay they've swallowed. This wad is called cud. They chew their cud a second time and swallow it again. When a cow has a baby, she makes milk for her calf, and the extra milk is sold for people to drink.

Baby **cats** are called kittens. Cats like to keep themselves very clean, and kittens begin to wash themselves when they're about four weeks old. Sometimes they use their rough tongues to lick their fur, other times they lick one paw to apply saliva, then they wipe the paw over their face or body, like the way we might use a wash cloth.

Baby **horses** are called foals. Horses have a hard covering on each foot called a hoof. To help protect their hooves and make them last longer as they gallop or trot, people put U-shaped metal rims called horseshoes onto the rims of a horse's hooves. Horses have helped farmers plow fields and pull carts to markets for thousands of years.

Baby **mice** are called pups. Mice are rodents that can be found on farms worldwide. They often build nests in the hay and hide there, away from cats, dogs, hawks, owls, and other animals that would eat them. At night they scurry along the ground looking for grain, seeds, and other food to eat.

Baby **owls** are called owlets. Barn owls often live in holes in trees, and sometimes in barn lofts and other human structures. They are active at night and rely on their excellent hearing as they fly silently to make a surprise attack on rats, mice, and voles. Farmers like owls because they act as a natural pest control.

Baby **turkeys** are called poults. Turkeys are farm birds raised for their meat all year round, not just at Thanksgiving. During the mating season, the males (toms) strut to attract females by fanning out their tail feathers and dragging their wings along the ground. Sometimes poults seem to be strutting too.

Baby **ducks** are called ducklings. Ducks are called waterfowl because they're often found at farm ponds or other bodies of water. The white American Pekin duck is a common farm duck. Their webbed feet act like paddles when swimming, but cause the ducks to waddle when walking. Ducklings follow their mother in a line.

Baby **pigs** are called piglets. Pigs have sensitive skin with very little hair to protect it, and they are also unable to sweat to regulate their temperature. They roll in mud to cool off and to cover their skin so it doesn't get sunburned. Muddy water evaporates slower than pure water, so the mud acts as natural sunblock. Unlike most animals, pigs designate a special area far away from their food and living areas for their "toilet."

Roosters have been on farms throughout history. A rooster, as shown in this story, is a male chicken. Roosters are famous for their early morning crowing (cock-a-doodle-do). But, in fact, they will crow at any time throughout the day. Farms usually have many hens, but just one rooster. He mates with most or all of the female hens (chickens) on the farm, ensuring an ongoing supply of fertile eggs. Hens can still lay eggs if there is no rooster, but the eggs will not hatch. A rooster often sits on a high lookout perch and serves as a guard, warning the hens when he senses danger. He also calls his hens when he has found a food source.

More Fun on the Farm

MATH

These two activities use plastic eggs. Twelve eggs is a good number to begin with for young children, but for older children you may want to use up to twenty eggs.

Subtraction: Place plastic eggs in a basket and appoint one child to be a "farmer." Give the basket to the "farmer" and have the farmer count the eggs and tell the class how many there are. The farmer takes out one or two eggs and asks the class how many are left. The first student who identifies the correct number becomes the farmer. The game continues with each new farmer taking out one, two, or three eggs until none are left.

Addition: Show the class plastic eggs in a box. Take out two eggs and place them in a basket. Appoint a child to be a "hen." Have the hen select one, two, or three eggs from the box and add them to the basket. The student who correctly identifies how many eggs are now in the basket becomes the next hen. The game continues until all of the eggs are out of the box and in the basket.

SCIENCE

Touch and Tell: Bring in various fruits and vegetables that are grown on a farm. Put them in a big pail and have children try to guess what they are by feeling them. No peeking!

Grow Your Own Bean: Dampen a paper towel with water, crumple it up, and put it in a clear plastic cup. Push a lima bean down the side of the cup. Keep the paper towel continuously moist, and watch the bean grow! Young children will be fascinated to watch the roots shooting down and tiny leaves emerging.

Plants from a Carrot Top: Cut the top off a carrot (about 2 inches). Stick a toothpick into either side of the carrot stump and rest it on top of a small glass filled with water so that the bottom of the carrot stump is touching the water. Keep the water touching the edge of the stump. Explain to children that a carrot is a root and it will not grow more carrots, but it will grow pretty fern-like leaves—a carrot top.

Birds and Eggs: Ask children to name all of the birds in the story—chicken (rooster or hen), owl, turkey, and duck. Draw or cut out pictures of these birds' actual eggs. Have children compare the eggs by size, shape, and color. Include other eggs to compare, such as an ostrich egg (largest egg) or a hummingbird egg (smallest egg).

LANGUAGE ARTS

Rhyme and Repetition: Practice listening skills by reading a page and asking the children to listen for the word that rhymes with the number: one/sun, two/chew, three/bee, four/floor, five/thrive, six/chicks, seven/heaven, eight/gate, nine/line, ten/den. Then ask them what words were repeated on every page.

Word and Number Matching: Write numerals 1 through 10 on index cards. On another set of index cards write the words "one" through "ten." Have children match the cards.

ART

Seasons: Fold a piece of 8" x 10" white paper into four quarters. Each section is a different season of the year: spring, summer, autumn and winter, in that order. Ask children to draw a picture of what would be happening on the farm during each season. Have them include different animals for each season.

Muddy Pigs: Cut out pig shapes from pink construction paper. Have children glue the pink pigs onto brown paper. Create "mud" by mixing a little brown paint into some shaving cream. Give each child a small cup of "mud" and a paint brush and have them cover their pigs in mud, or use brown markers or crayons instead of paint.

Farm Chores: Give children a white paper plate and have them draw two lines to create four quarters. In each quarter, have children draw what they think the farmer does every day. For example, collecting eggs, milking a cow, feeding the pigs, lassoing a horse, fixing the barn, riding a tractor, building a gate, sowing seeds, or plowing fields.

FROM FARM TO TABLE

Homemade Butter: Pour heavy cream in a jar and secure the lid very tightly. Then shake, shake, shake! You can make one container of butter using a large mason jar and pass it around so each child has a turn to shake. Or you can use baby food jars to give children their own individual container. In a large jar, it will take about twenty minutes for the milk to solidify. Baby food jars take about ten minutes. Sing some farm songs while you shake. The process is complete when you have a fairly solid mass at the bottom of the jar. Pour off the buttermilk. If you like, stir in some kosher salt before spreading the butter on crackers.

Honey Corn: Children can also use their homemade butter with this recipe from *What's in the Garden?* also by Marianne Berkes. With an adult, remove husks and silk from four ears of corn. Fill a large pot half full with water and bring to a boil. Stir in 2 tbsp. of honey and then drop in the corn. Cook three to four minutes. Lift the corn out of the water with tongs and drain on paper towels. Serve with butter, salt, and pepper.

Movement and Music

Animals in the Barn: Put a big hoop down on the floor and tell the children it's a pretend barn. Ask a child to step into the "barn" and become one of the animals from the book. Explain that as they leave the barn (step out of the hoop) they will act out how the animal moves. Emphasize that they can use actions but no sounds. For example, the horse could gallop, the duck could waddle, the owl could fly, etc. Help children really think about how their animal moves by asking questions, such as, "Does the animal walk on all fours?" "Does it use its tail?" Have the rest of the class guess what animal is being acted out. The child who guesses correctly is the next person in the "barn."

Stand Up, Sit Down: Use colored construction paper and have children draw and cut out one of the baby animals from this book. Tape the cutouts to straws or craft sticks. Make sure children can identify the baby animal on their stick, then have them follow your directions to stand up or sit down. For example, say:

1. Chicks stand up.
2. Calves and kittens stand up.
3. Foals stand up.

4. Chicks and kittens sit down.
5. Piglets stand up.
6. Foals sit down.

Continue using all of the baby animals. The game is over when there is only one baby animal standing! You can also do this activity with the types of fruits and vegetables grown on the farm. Use colored construction paper and have children draw and cut out common foods, such as corn (yellow), pumpkins (orange), beans (green), apples (red), etc.

Adapt a Song: Sing about farm animal babies using the tune to "The Wheels on the Bus." In each verse, include the name of the baby, the sound it makes, and where the babies are in this story. For example:

The chicks on the ground go cheep cheep cheep.

Cheep, cheep, cheep.

Cheep, cheep, cheep.

The chicks on the ground go cheep, cheep, cheep

All around the farm.

The kids in the grass go maa, maa, maa.

The calves in the pasture go moo, moo, moo.

The kittens on the floor go mew, mew, mew

The foals in the field go neigh, neigh, neigh.

And so on.

Marianne Berkes has spent much of her life as an early childhood educator, children's theater director, and children's librarian. She is the award-winning author of over twenty-three interactive picture books that make learning fun. Her books, inspired by her love of nature, open kids' eyes to the magic found in our natural world. Ever since she wrote *Over in the Ocean*, teachers and students have suggested she write *Over on the Farm*. But she was busy researching for her other "Over" habitat books, including *Jungle*, *Arctic*, *Australia*, *Forest*, *River*, *Mountain*, and finally, *Grasslands*. Now that her "Over" habitat books are complete, *Over on the Farm* has become a reality. Marianne hopes young children will want to read it again and again, each time learning something new and exciting. Her website is MarianneBerkes.com.

Cathy Morrison is an award-winning illustrator in Colorado who grew up spending most summers on her family farm in Texas. The farm included many cows, two horses, several pigs, and no chickens, but there was one peacock. She began her career in animation and graphic design, but discovered her passion for children's book illustration while raising her two children. After several years illustrating with traditional media, she now works digitally, which helps publishers adapt the art into interactive book apps.

To the Vanderslice family with love from Mama M.
And for Sandy and her chickens.
—MB

To a girl named Owen.
—CM

Text © 2016, 2021 by Marianne Berkes
Illustrations © 2016, 2021 by Cathy Morrison
Cover and internal design © 2021 by Sourcebooks
Cover and internal image © lukbar/Getty Images
Series design by Kelley Lanuto

Published by Dawn Publications, an imprint of Sourcebooks eXplore
P.O. Box 4410, Naperville, Illinois 60567–4410
(630) 961-3900
sourcebookskids.com

Originally published in 2016 in the United States by Dawn Publications.

Library of Congress Cataloging-in-Publication Data is on file with the publisher.

Source of Production: Wing King Tong Paper Products Co. Ltd., Shenzhen, Guangdong Province, China
Date of Production: July 2021
Run Number: 5021470
Printed and bound in China.
WKT 10 9 8 7 6 5 4 3 2 1

ALSO BY MARIANNE BERKES AND DAWN PUBLICATIONS

Baby on Board: How Animal Parents Carry their Young — These are some of the clever ways animals carry their babies!

Over in the Ocean — With unique and outstanding style, this book portrays a vivid community of marine creatures.

Over in the Jungle — As with *Ocean*, this book captures a rain forest teeming with remarkable animals.

Over in the Arctic — Another charming counting rhyme introduces creatures of the tundra.

Over in the Forest — Follow the tracks of forest animals, but watch out for the skunk!

Over in Australia — Australian animals are often unique, many with pouches for the babies. Such fun!

Over in a River — Beavers, manatees, and so many more animals help teach the geography and habitats of ten great North American rivers.

Over on a Mountain — Twenty cool animals, ten great mountain ranges, and seven continents, all in one story!

Over in the Grasslands — Come along on a safari! Lions, rhinos, and hippos introduce the African Savanna.

Over on a Desert — Camels, tortoises, roadrunners, and jerboas help teach the habitat of the desert.

Going Around the Sun: Some Planetary Fun — Earth is part of a fascinating "family" of planets.

Going Home: The Mystery of Animal Migration — A book that is an introduction to animals that migrate.

Seashells by the Seashore — Kids discover, identify, and count twelve beautiful shells to give Grandma for her birthday.

The Swamp Where Gator Hides — Still as a log, only his watchful eyes can be seen.

What's in the Garden? — Good food doesn't begin on a store shelf in a box. It comes from a garden bursting with life!

OTHER NATURE BOOKS FROM DAWN PUBLICATIONS

Tall Tall Tree — Take a peek at some of the animals that make their home in a tall, tall tree—a magnificent coast redwood. Rhyming verses and a one-to-ten counting scheme made this a real page-turner.

Daytime Nighttime, All Through the Year — Delightful rhymes depict two animals for each month, one active during the day and one busy at night. See all the action!

Octopus Escapes Again! — Swim along with Octopus as she searches for food. Will she eat or be eaten? She outwits dangerous enemies by using a dazzling display of defenses.

Paddle, Perch, Climb: Bird Feet Are Neat — Become a bird detective as you meet the feet that help birds eat—so many different shapes, sizes, and ways to use them. It's time for lunch!

Dandelion Seed's Big Dream — A charming tale that follows a seed as it floats from the countryside to the city and encounters all sorts of obstacles and opportunities.

A Moon of My Own — An adventurous young girl journeys around the world accompanied by her faithful companion, the Moon. Wonder and beauty await you.